CW00919373

Pocket
AUDREY
HEPBURN WISDOM

Pocket
AUDREY
HEPBURN WISDOM

—Inspirational quotes from a Hollywood legend—

Hardie Grant

BOOKS

CONTENTS

AUDREY'S KISSES

My mother, Audrey Hepburn, dreamt as a child. She dreamt of going back to school, of skating on the frozen waterways of Holland, of playing outside. She dreamt of when the war would end, of her father coming home, of a family of her own. And she dreamt of performing.

And when the dream of becoming a performer came true, at the tender age of 23, she lived life to the fullest, tasting its every morsel, like only those who have known real hunger are able to. Starved of a formal education, she read every day of her life. She didn't take it for granted. She knew it was the expression of freedom, the exercise of democracy – a luxury. She loved languages and spoke six. She studied diction. Listened to people. She wrote. Loved words. Sang them. She was mindful of others and put herself in their shoes – and thought before opening her mouth.

These quotes emerged over time – the smooth stones of a life devoid of half truths. Born out of a sparkling clarity, with time, they became words of wisdom. If a smile is the purification of laughter, then these are kisses from Audrey's mind.

– Sean Hepburn Ferrer

Family &
FRIENDS

_____

"True friends are families which you can select."

_____

———————————————

"You can tell more about
a person by what he
says about others than
you can by what others
say about him."

———————————————

_____

"I had to make a choice
at one point in my life,
of missing films or
missing my children...

_____

It was a very easy
decision to make because
I missed my children so
very much."

_____

"I may not always
be offered work, but I'll
always have my family."

_____

"When you have nobody
you can make a cup of
tea for, when nobody
needs you, that's when
I think life is over."

_____

"I love people who make me laugh. I honestly think it's the thing I like most, to laugh…

_____

––––––––––––––––––––––

It cures a multitude
of ills. It's probably the
most important thing
in a person."

––––––––––––––––––––––

Life &
LAUGHTER

"Living is like tearing
through a museum.
Not until later do you really
start absorbing what you
saw, thinking about it
and remembering."

"I decided, very early on, just to accept life unconditionally; I never expected it to do anything special for me, yet I seemed to accomplish far more than I had ever hoped."

"My own life has been much more than a fairy tale. I've had my share of difficult moments, but whatever difficulties I've gone through, I've always gotten the prize at the end."

"Pick the day. Enjoy it – to the hilt. The day as it comes. People as they come."

"The past has helped me appreciate the present – and I don't want to spoil any of it by fretting about the future."

"I heard a definition once: happiness is health and a short memory! I wish I'd invented it, because it is very true."

"I believe, every day,
you should have at least
one exquisite moment."

"Nothing is impossible,
the word itself says
'I'm possible'!"

"Good things aren't supposed to just fall into your lap. God is very generous, but He expects you to do your part first."

"I believe that laughing is the best calorie burner."

"If my world were
to cave in tomorrow,
I would look back on all
the pleasures, excitements
and worthwhilenesses
I have been lucky enough
to have had…

Not the sadness,
not my miscarriages
or my father leaving
home, but the joy of
everything else. It will
have been enough."

Beauty &
ELEGANCE

"There are certain shades of limelight that can wreck a girl's complexion."

"Elegance is the only beauty that never fades."

———————

"The beauty in a woman
is not in the clothes
she wears, the figure that
she carries, or the way
she combs her hair.
The beauty of a woman
is seen in her eyes…

———————

because that is the
doorway to her heart;
the place where love
resides. True beauty in
a woman is reflected
in her soul."

"A woman can be beautiful as well as intellectual."

"There are more important things than outward appearance. No amount of makeup can cover an ugly personality."

"I never thought I'd
land in pictures with
a face like mine."

"I believe that happy girls are the prettiest girls."

Humanity & CHARITY

"I have learnt how to live…
how to be in the world and
of the world, and not just to
stand aside and watch."

"Giving is living.
If you stop wanting to
give, there's nothing
more to live for."

"The 'Third World' is a term I don't like very much, because we're all one world. I want people to know that the largest part of humanity is suffering."

"I can testify to what UNICEF means to children, because I was among those who received food and medical relief right after World War II. I have a long-lasting gratitude and trust for what UNICEF does."

"A quality education has the power to transform societies in a single generation, provide children with the protection they need from the hazards…

of poverty, labor
exploitation and disease,
and given them the
knowledge, skills, and
confidence to reach their
full potential."

"Since the world has existed, there has been injustice. But it is 'One World', the more so as it becomes smaller, more accessible...

There is just no question that there is a moral obligation that those who have, should give to those who have nothing."

♥

LOVE

———————

"They say love is the
best investment; the more
you give, the more you
get in return."

———————

———————

"For me, the only
things of interest
are those linked
to the heart."

———————

———————————

"I believe in kissing,
kissing a lot."

———————————

"We all want to be loved,
don't we? Everyone looks
for a way of finding love.
It's a constant search
for affection in every
walk of life."

———————

"Whatever a man might do, whatever misery or heartache your children might give you…

———————

_____

however much your parents irritate you – it doesn't matter because you love them."

_____

"You can always tell what kind of a person a man really thinks you are by the earrings he gives you."

"I don't want to
be alone, I want to
be left alone."

Success &
CAREER

"Success is like reaching an important birthday and finding out you're exactly the same."

"It is too much to hope that I shall keep up my success. I don't ask for that. All I shall do is my best – and hope."

"I was asked to act when I couldn't act. I was asked to sing 'Funny Face' when I couldn't sing, and dance with Fred Astaire when I couldn't dance...

_____

and do all kinds of
things I wasn't prepared
for. Then I tried like
mad to cope with it."

_____

———————————

"I'm not a born actress, as such, I care about expressing feelings."

———————————

"Opportunities don't often come along. So, when they do, you have to grab them!"

———————

"People associate me
with a time when movies
were pleasant, when
women wore pretty dresses
in films and you heard
beautiful music…

———————

I always love it when
people write me and say
'I was having a rotten
time, and I walked into
a cinema and saw one of
your movies, and it made
such a difference.'"

―――――――――

"I probably hold the
distinction of being one
movie star who, by all logic,
should never have made it.
At each stage of my career,
I lacked the experience."

―――――――――

"I was born with something that appealed to an audience at that particular time... I acted instinctively. I've had one of the greatest schools of all – a whole row of great, great directors."

SELF

"Look, whenever I hear
or read I'm beautiful,
I simply don't understand
it… I'm certainly
not beautiful in any
conventional way.
I didn't make my career
on beauty."

"I was born with an enormous need for affection, and a terrible need to give it."

"When the chips are down, you are alone, and loneliness can be terrifying. Fortunately, I've always had a chum I could call…

And I love to be alone.
It doesn't bother
me one bit. I'm my
own company."

"I tried always to do better:
saw always a little further.
I tried to stretch myself."

———————————

"I've been lucky."

———————————

"Sex appeal is something that you feel deep down inside. It's suggested rather than shown. I'm not as well-stacked as Sophia Loren or Gina Lollobrigida, but there is more to…

---

sex appeal than just measurements. I don't need a bedroom to prove my womanliness. I can convey just as much sex appeal, picking apples off a tree or standing in the rain."

"There must be something wrong with those people who think Audrey Hepburn doesn't perspire, hiccup or sneeze, because they know that's not true. In fact, I hiccup more than most."

———————————

"I believe in being strong
when everything seems
to be going wrong."

———————————

Fashion & STYLE

"Life is a party.
Dress for it."

"Why change? Everyone has his own style. When you have found it, you should stick to it."

"My look is attainable. Women can look like Audrey Hepburn by flipping out their hair, buying the large sunglasses, and the little sleeveless dresses."

"I never think of myself as an icon. What is in other people's mind is not in my mind. I just do my thing."

"I believe in miracles."

"Paris is always a good idea."

"

For attractive lips, speak
words of kindness.

For lovely eyes, seek out
the good in people.

For a slim figure, share your
food with the hungry.

For beautiful hair, let a child run his
or her fingers through it once a day.

For poise, walk with the knowledge
you'll never walk alone.

People, even more than things,
have to be restored, renewed, revived…

reclaimed, and redeemed and
redeemed and redeemed.

Never throw out anybody.

Remember, if you ever need a helping hand,
you will find one at the end of your arm.

As you grow older, you will discover that
you have two hands, one for helping yourself,
the other for helping others.

99

*Quotes from Sam Levenson's letter to his
granddaughter used in Audrey's UNICEF speeches.*

Published in 2020 by Hardie Grant Books,
an imprint of Hardie Grant Publishing

Hardie Grant Books (London)
5th & 6th Floors
52–54 Southwark Street
London SE1 1UN

Hardie Grant Books (Melbourne)
Building 1, 658 Church Street
Richmond, Victoria 3121

hardiegrantbooks.com

British Library Cataloguing-in-Publication Data. A catalogue record for this book
is available from the British Library.

Pocket Audrey Hepburn Wisdom

ISBN: 978-1-78488-361-4

10 9 8 7 6 5 4 3 2 1

Publishing Director: Kate Pollard
Editor: Eila Purvis
Designer: Studio Noel
Illustrator: Julia Murray

Colour reproduction by p2d
Printed and bound in China by Leo Paper Products Ltd.